I0497854

FIRST NAME:

....

LAST NAME:

....

TEST
COLOR

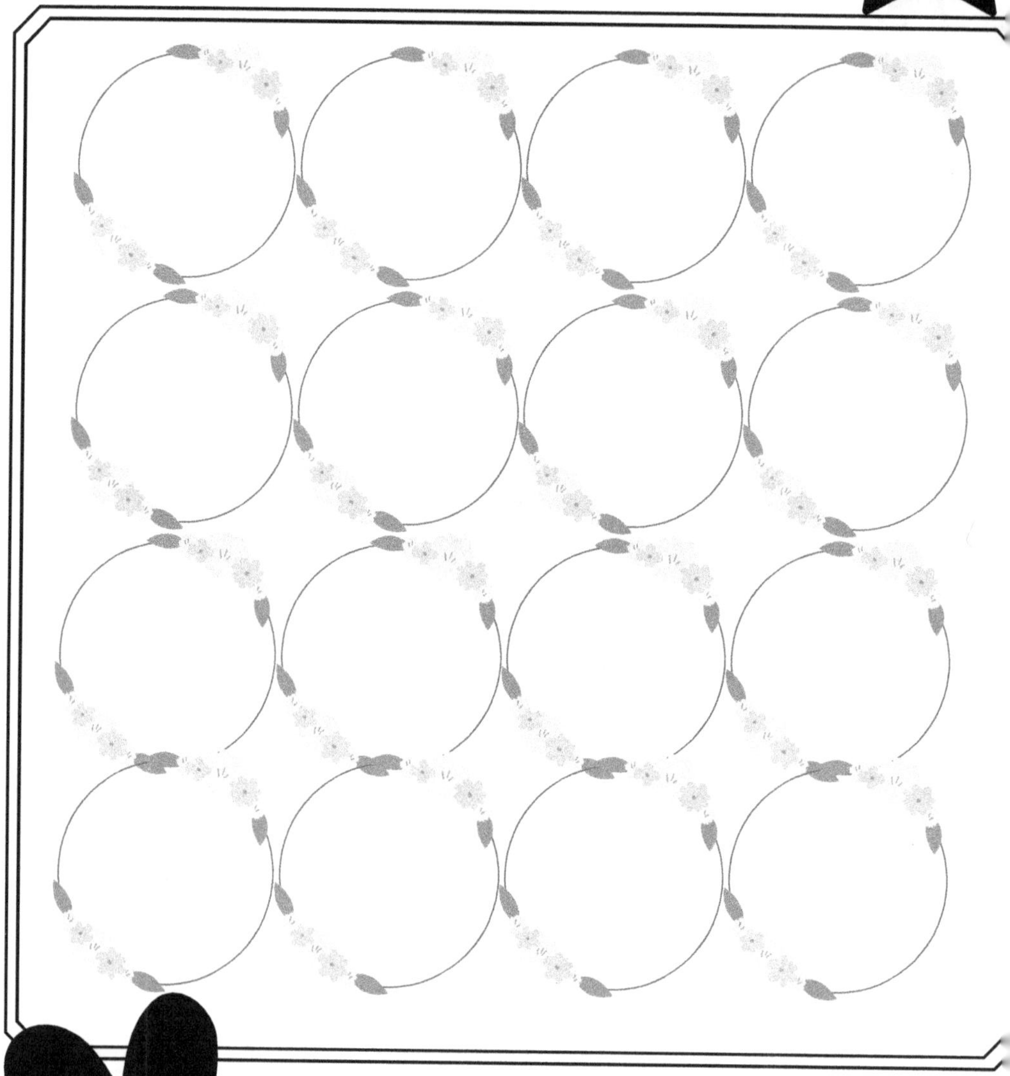

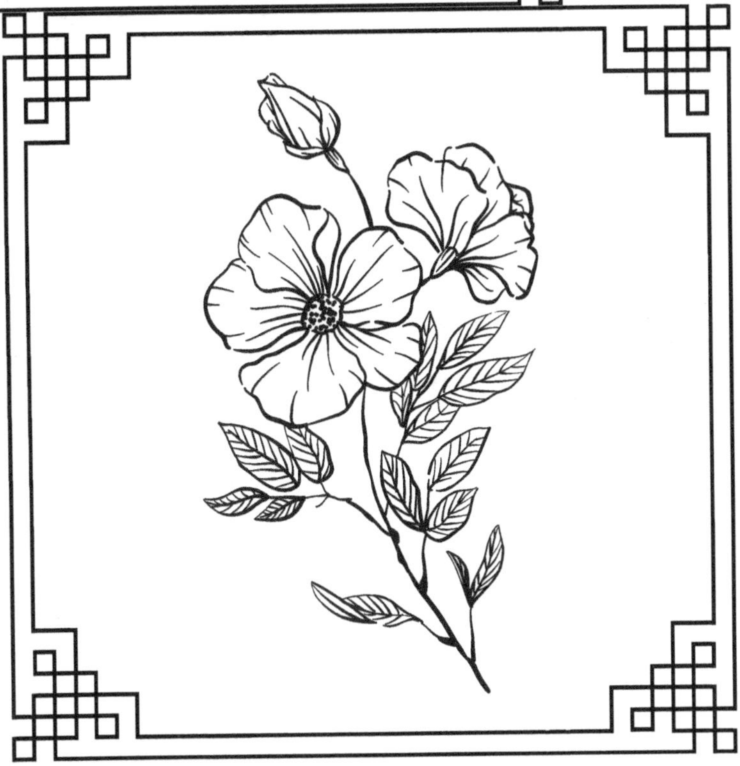

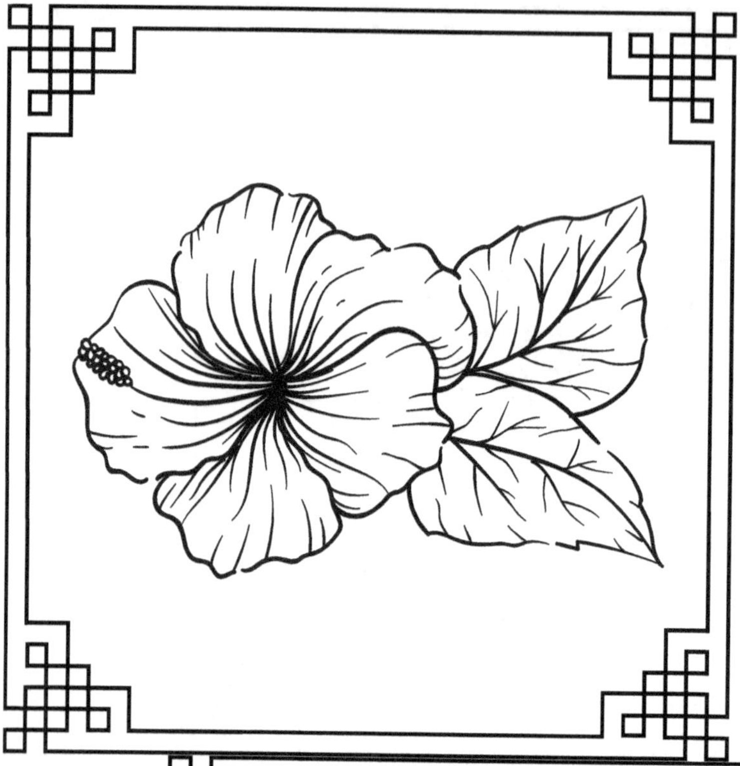

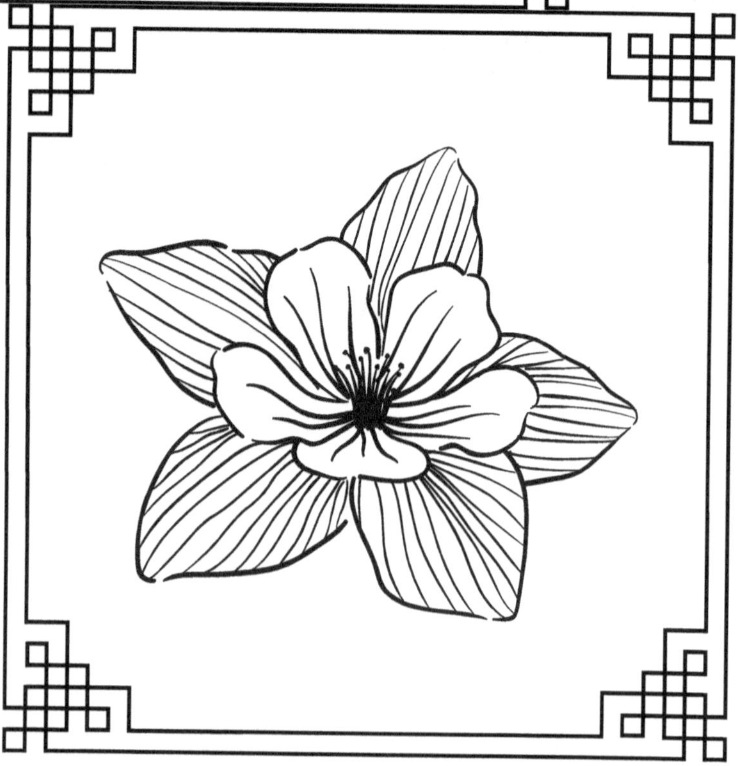

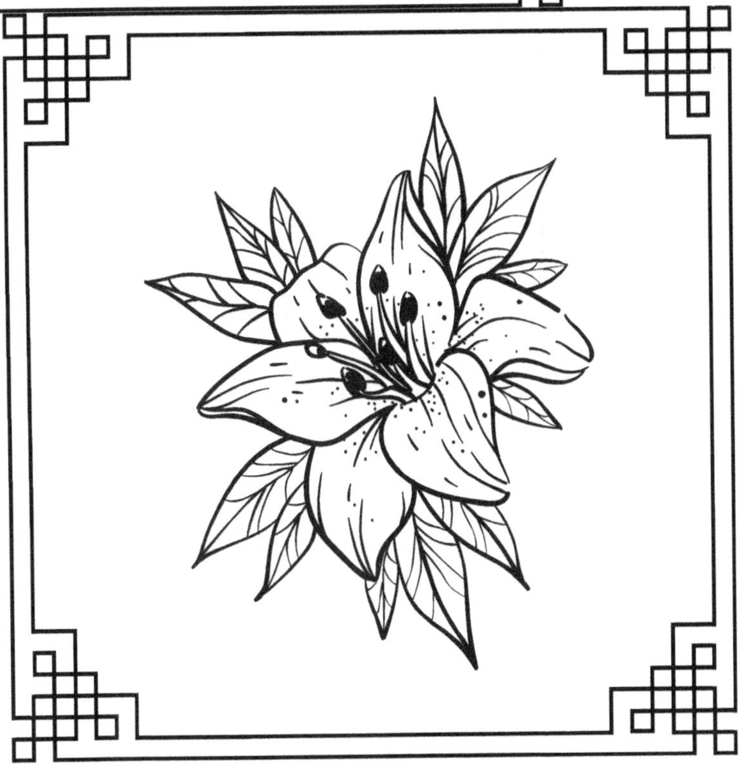

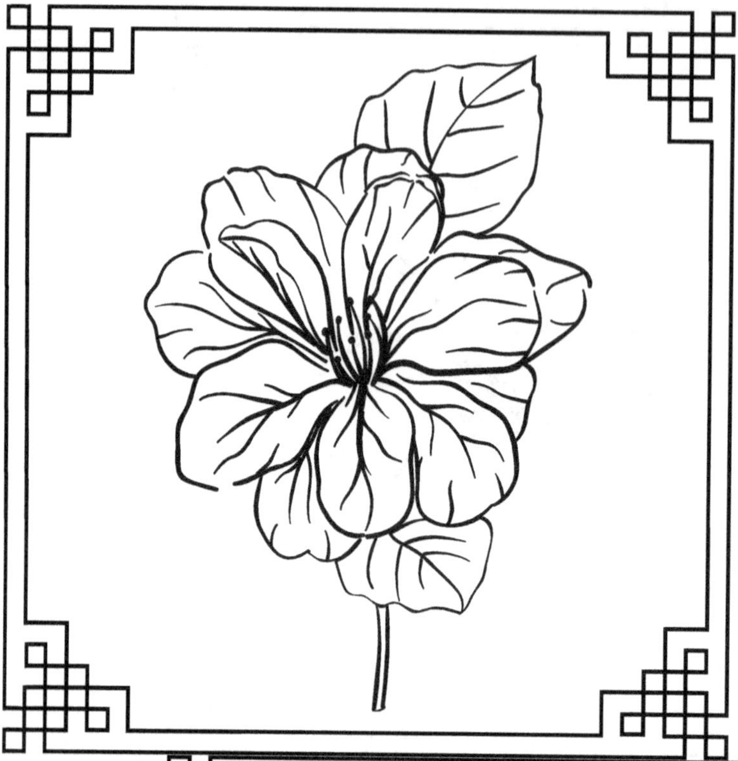

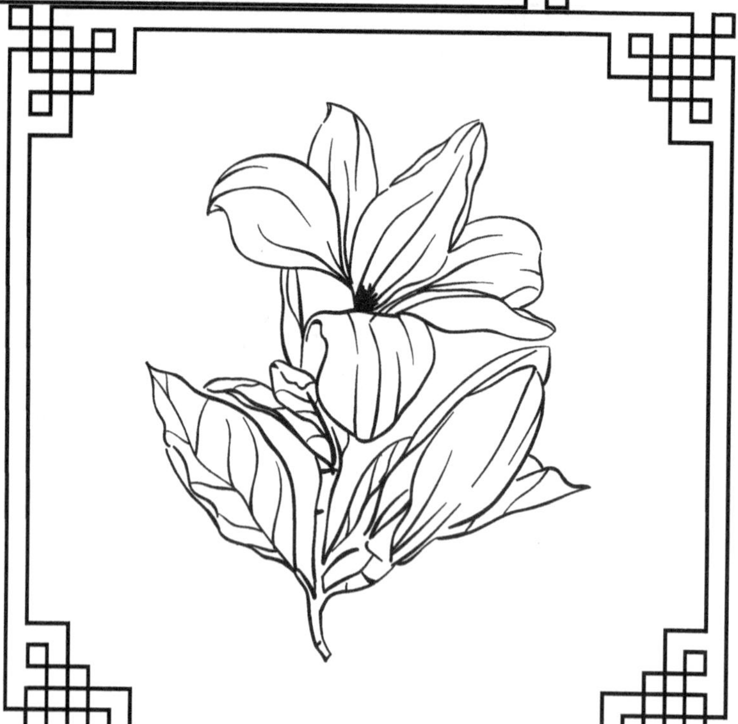

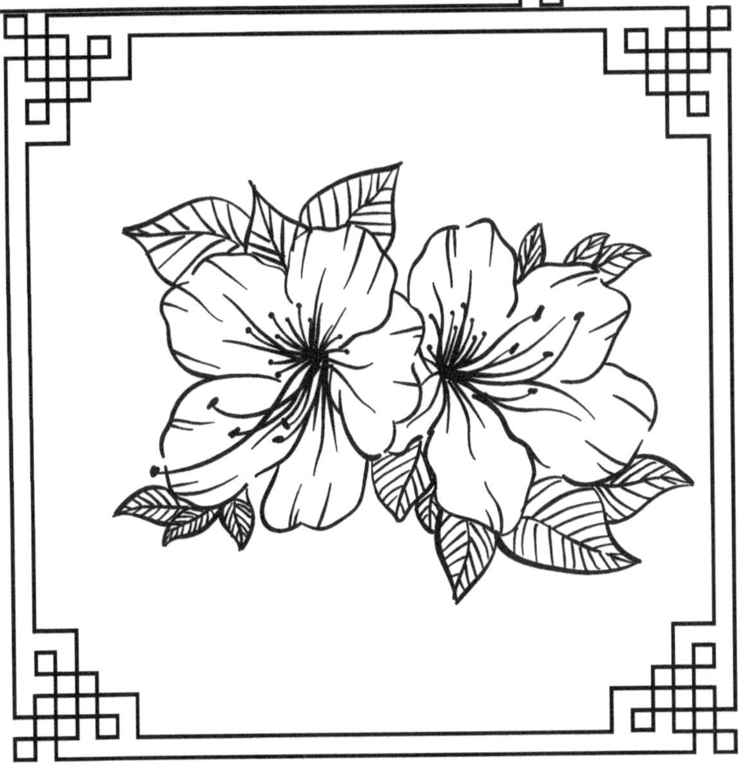

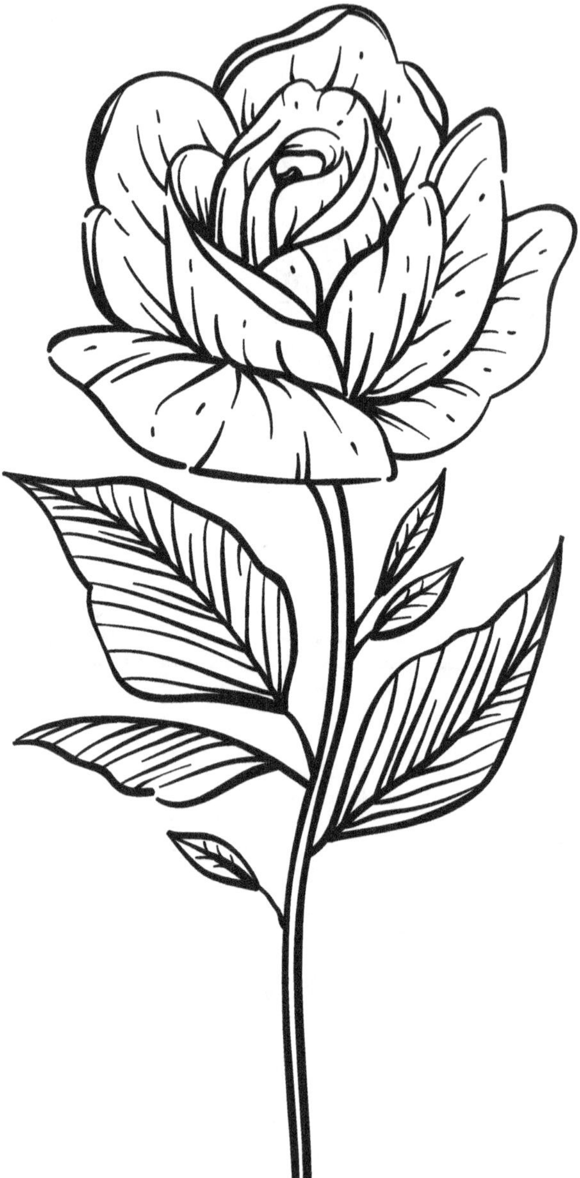

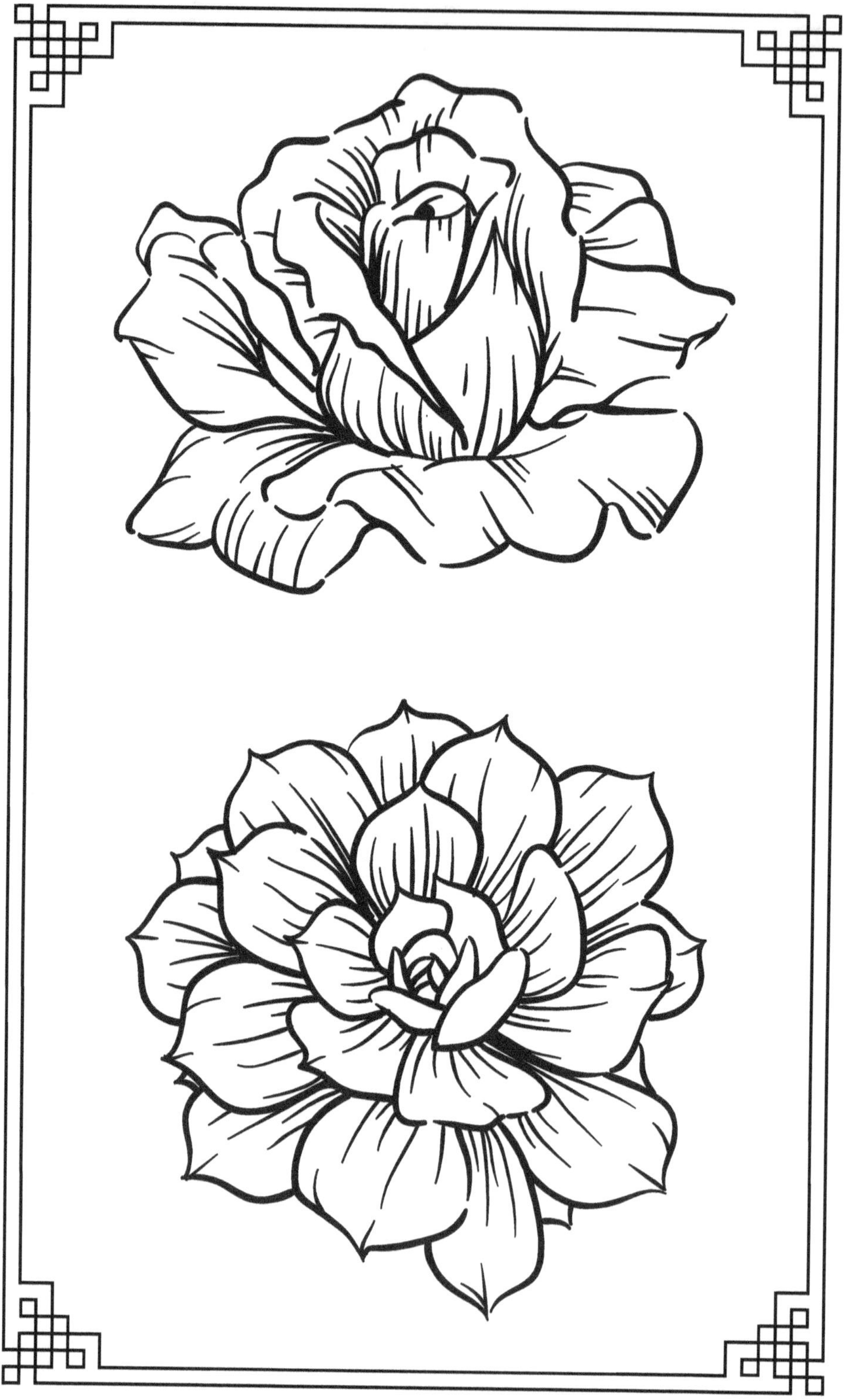

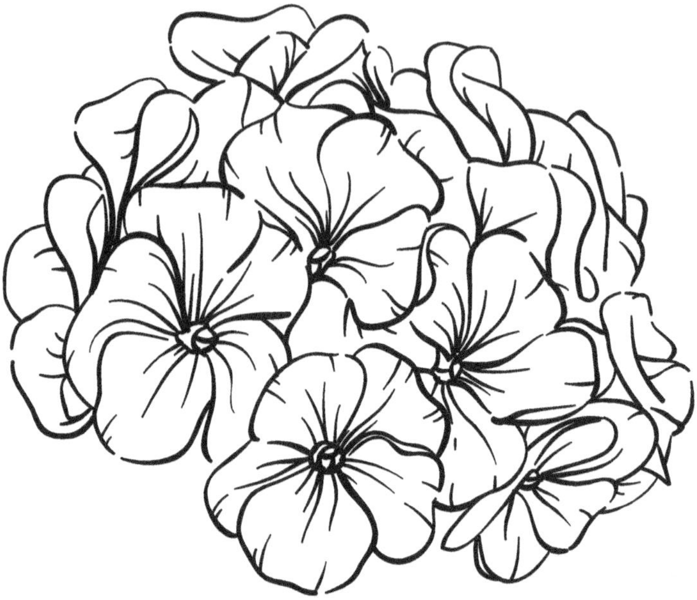

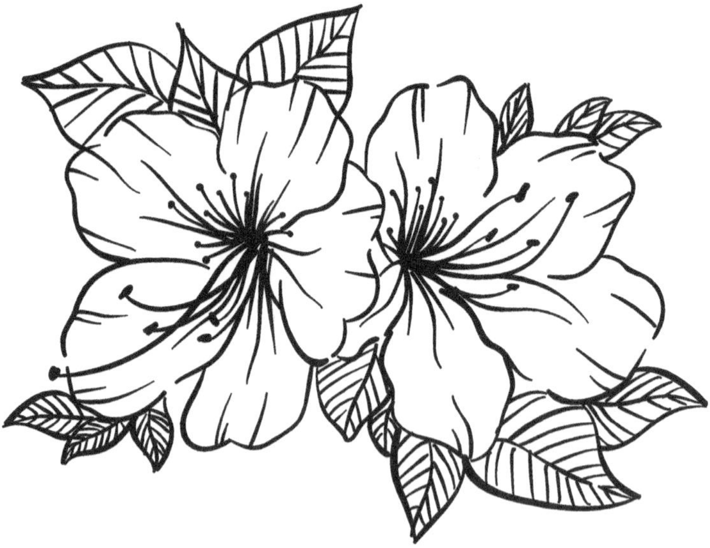

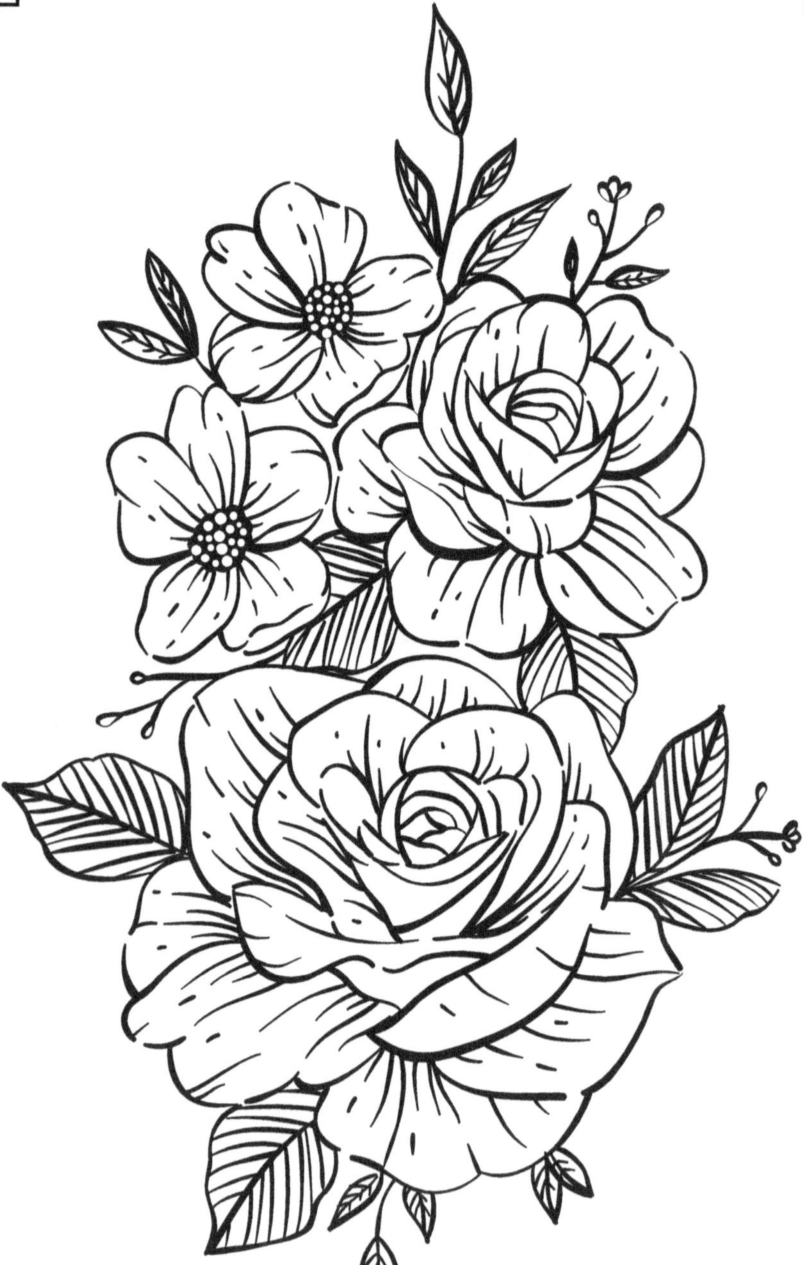

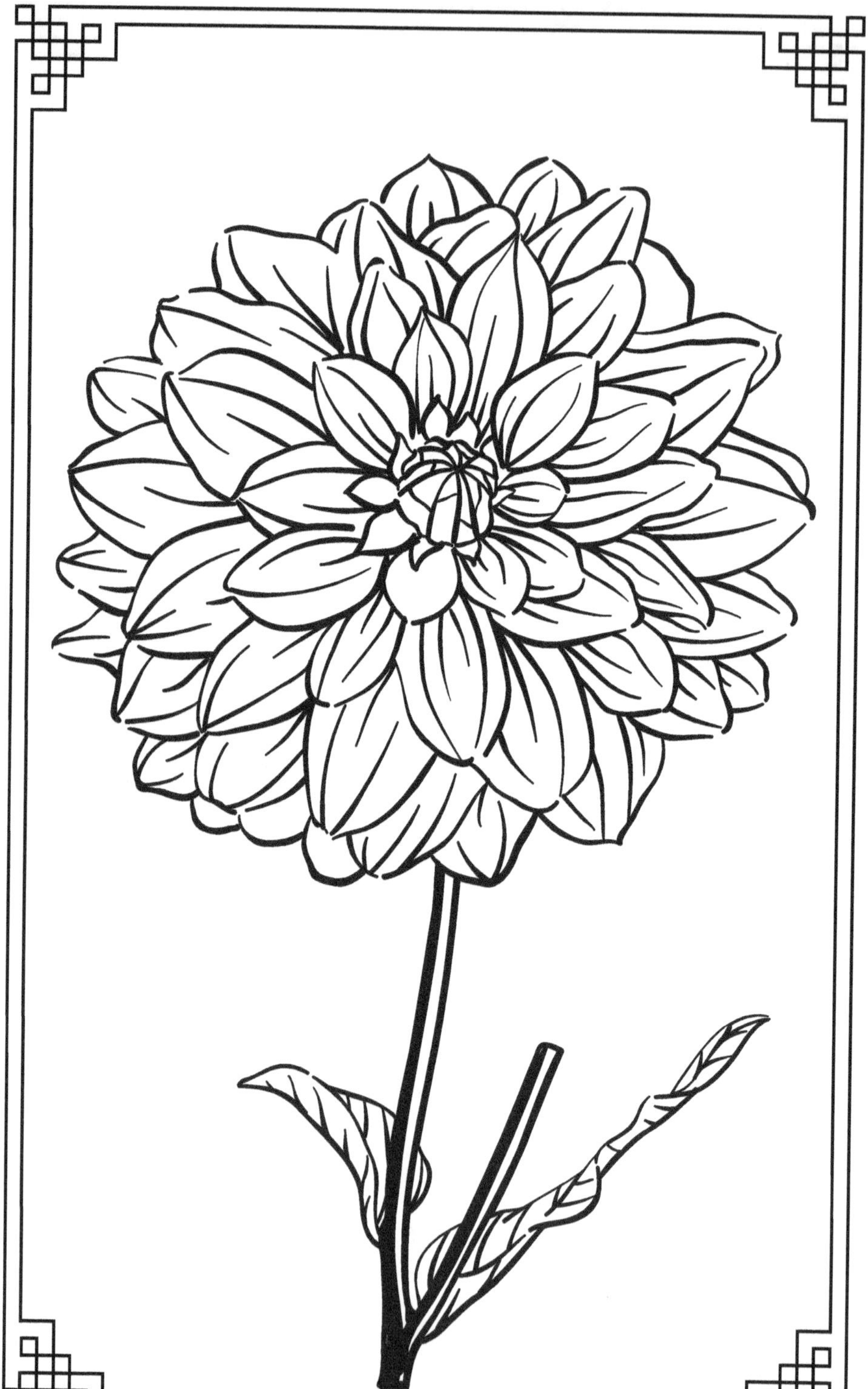

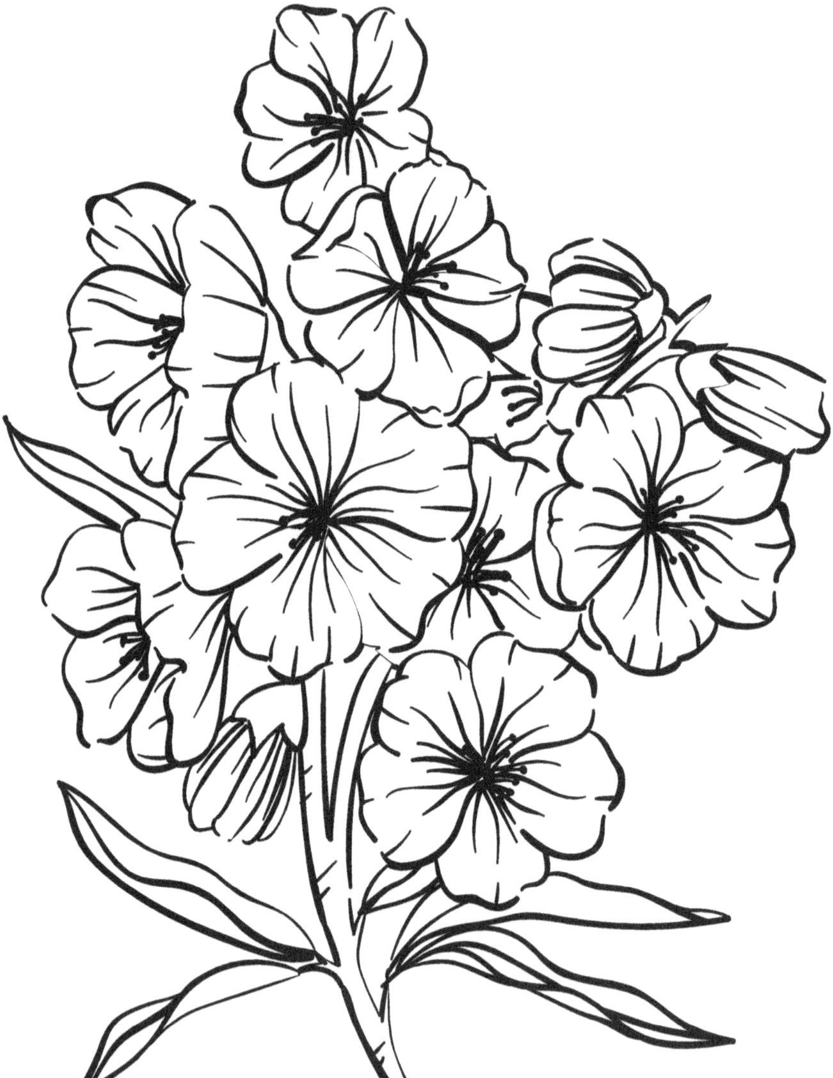

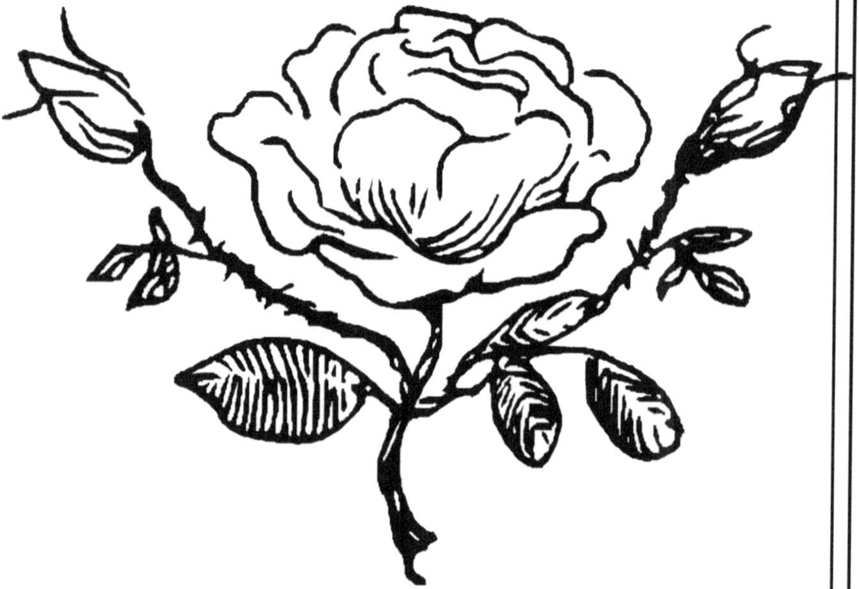

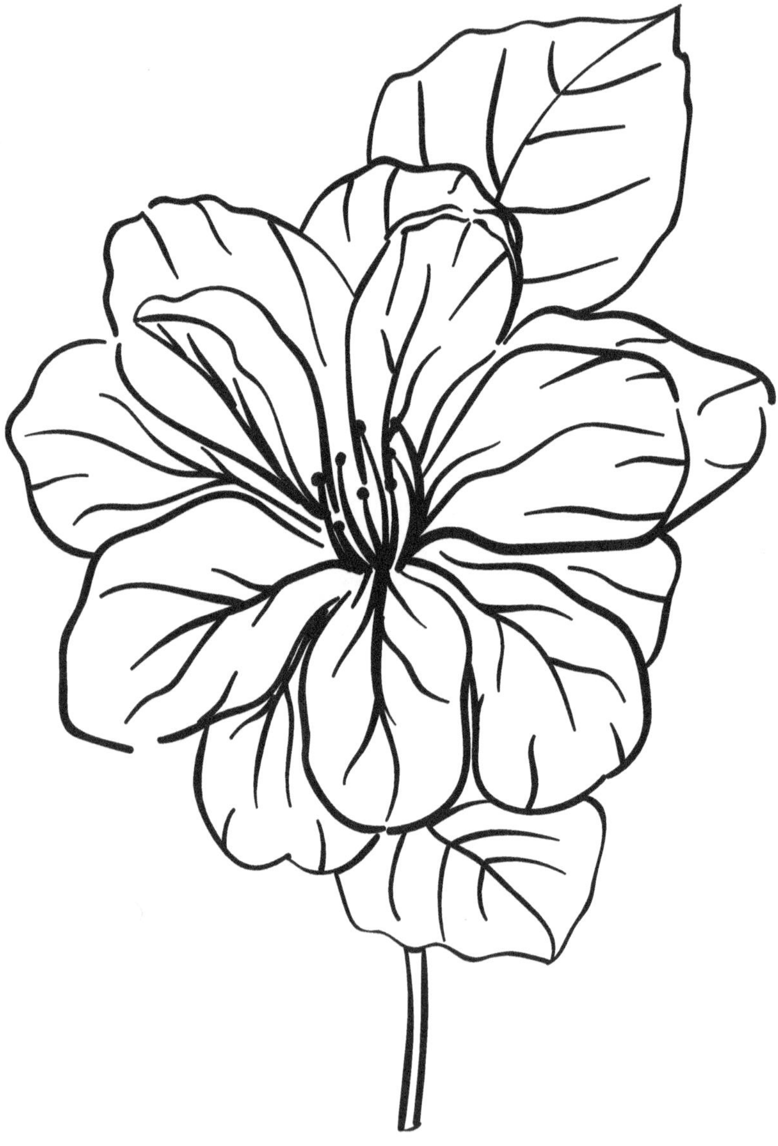

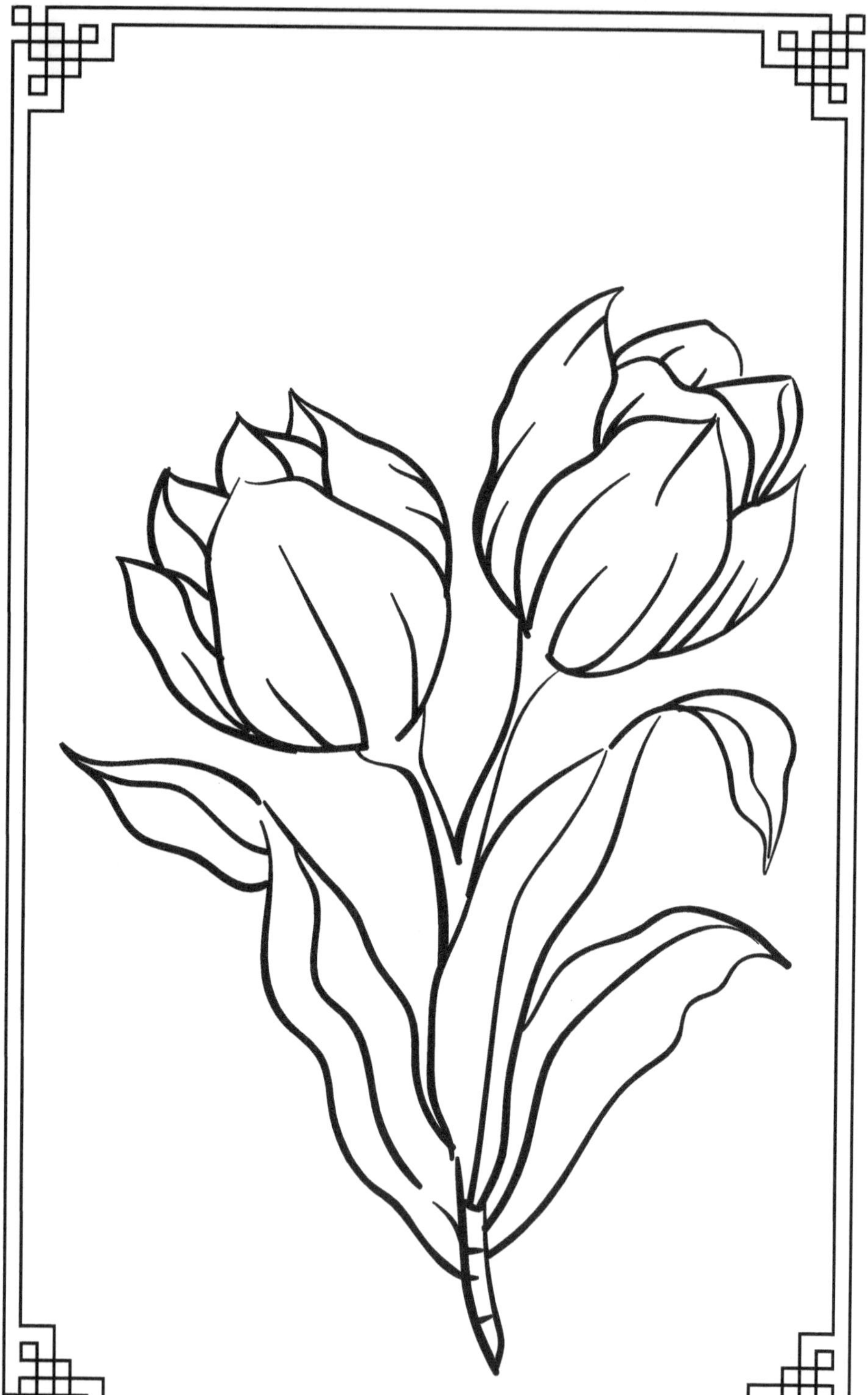

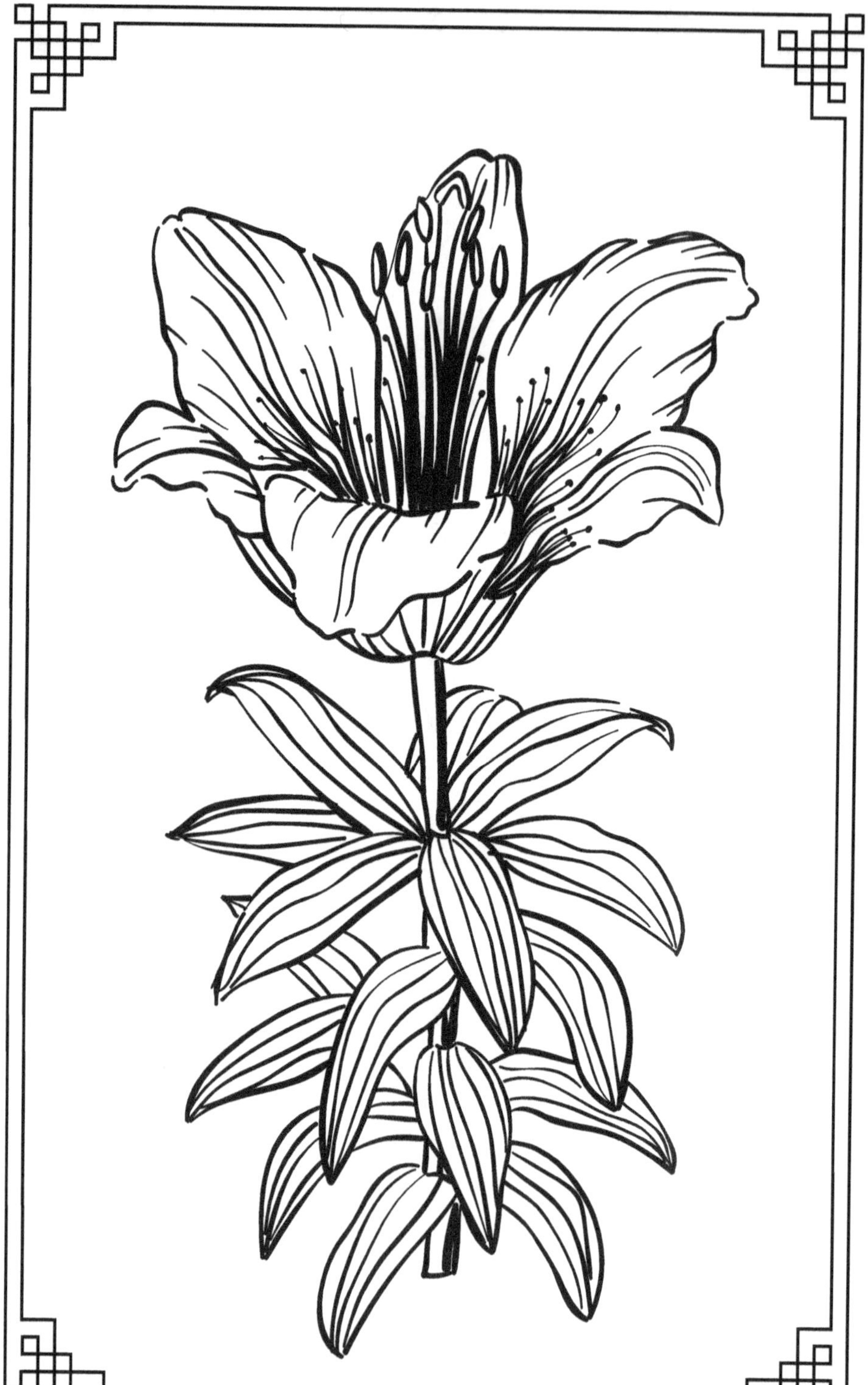

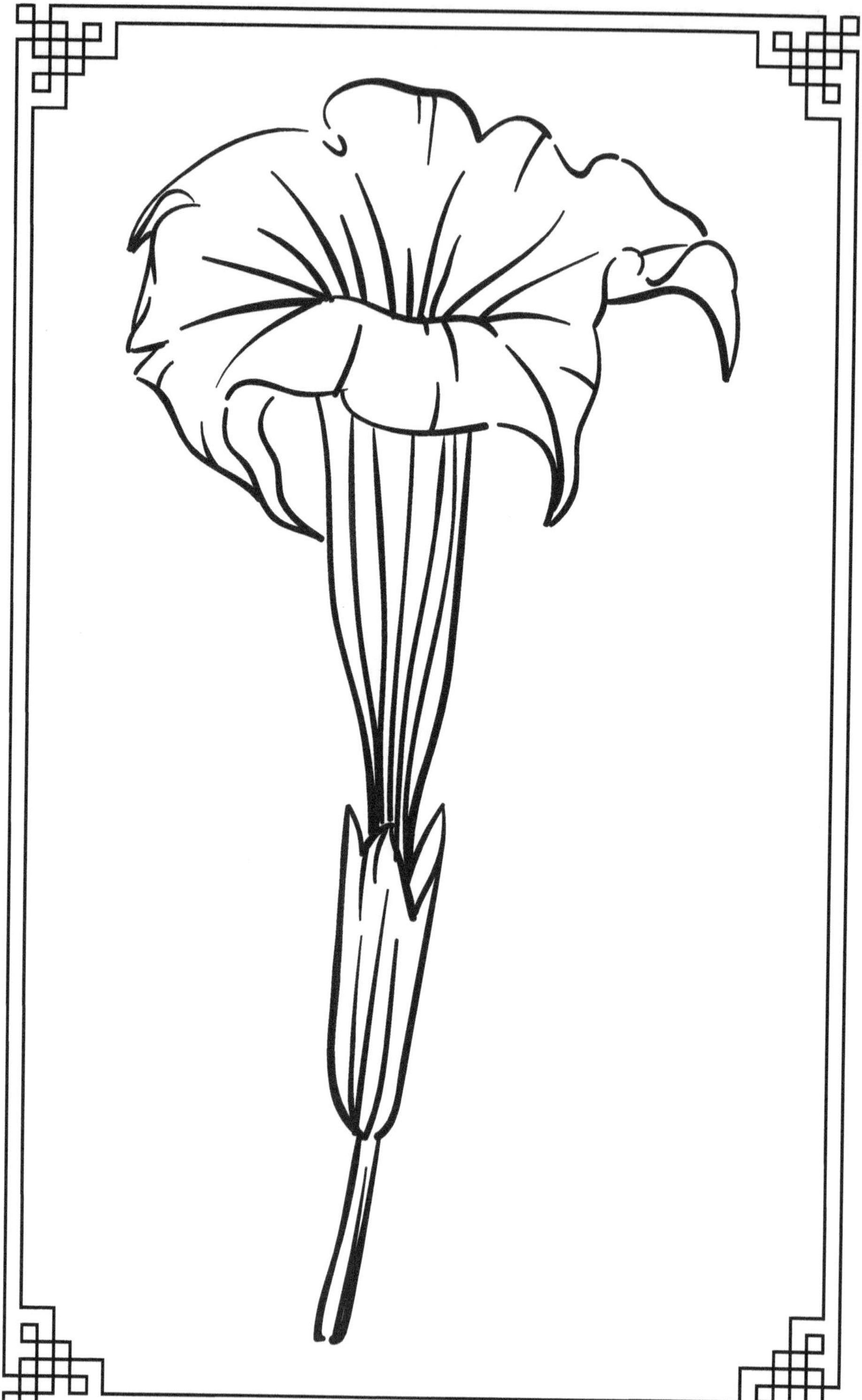

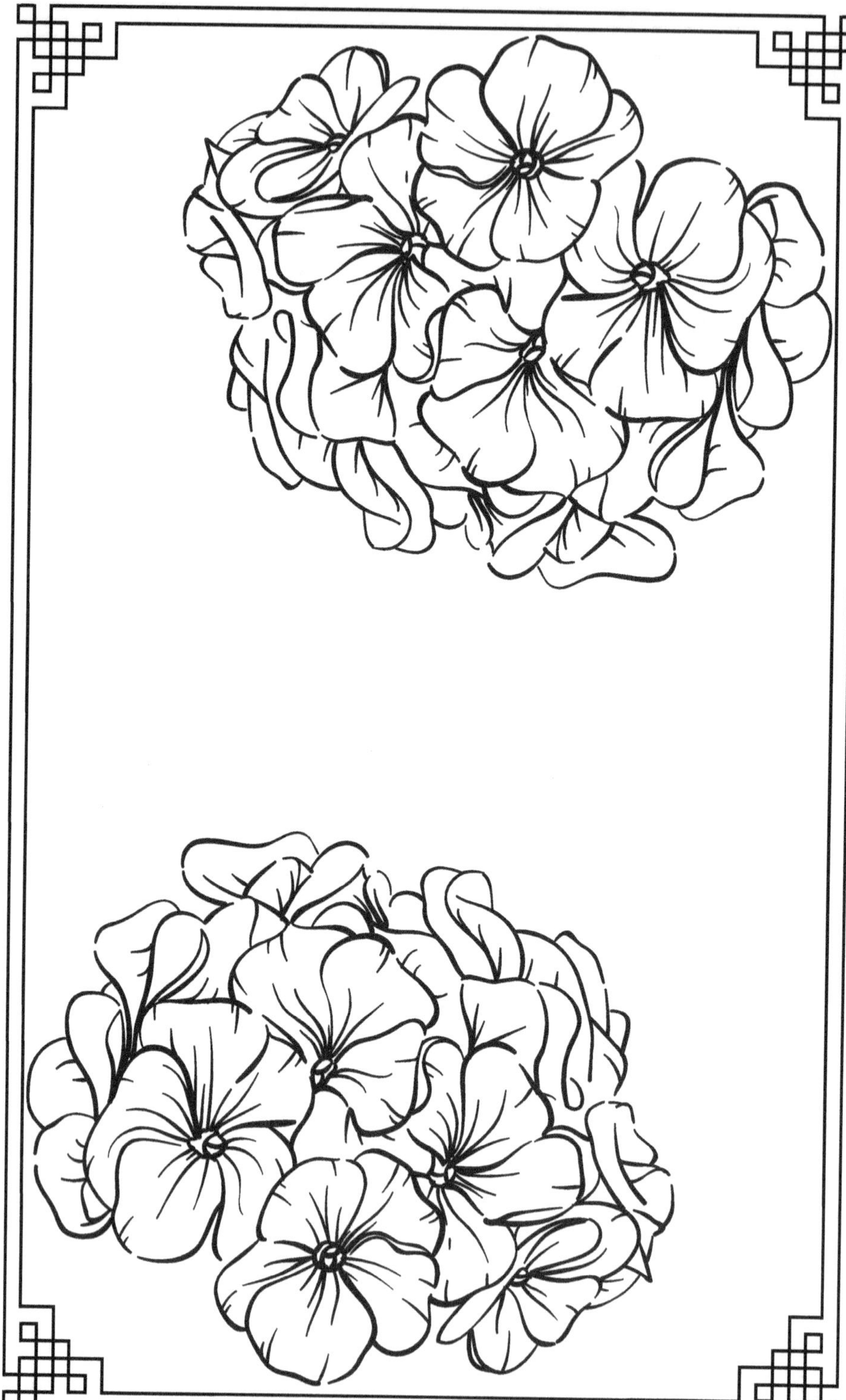

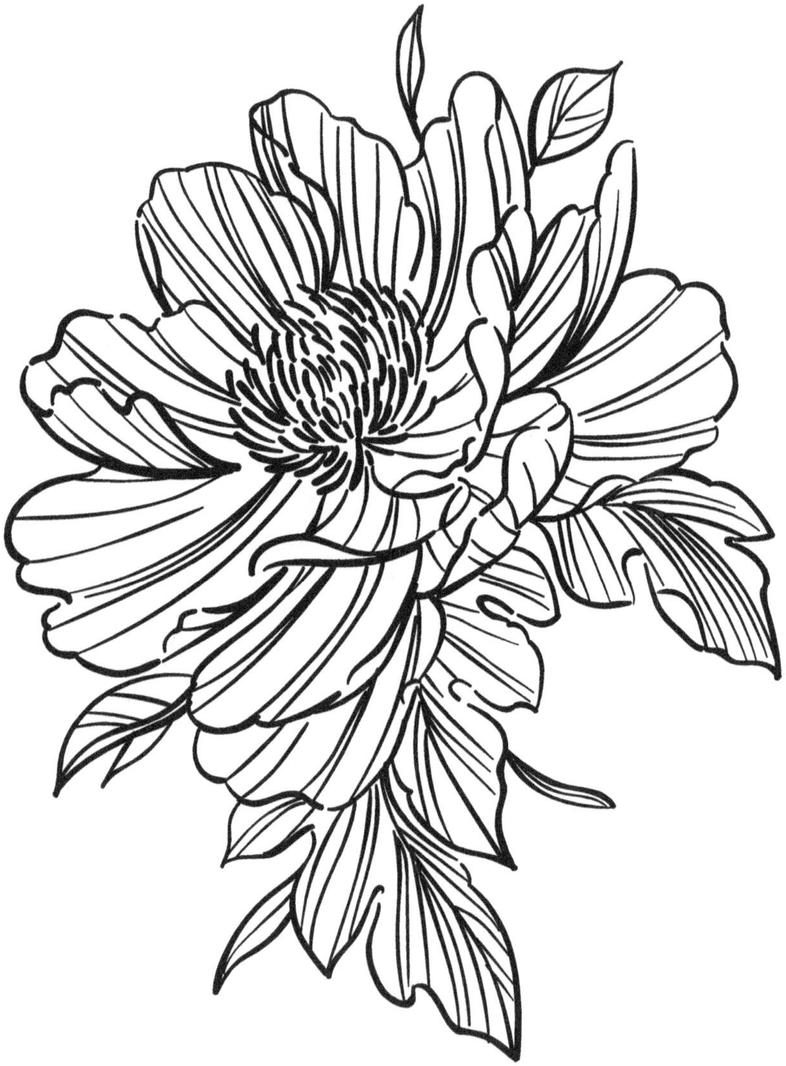

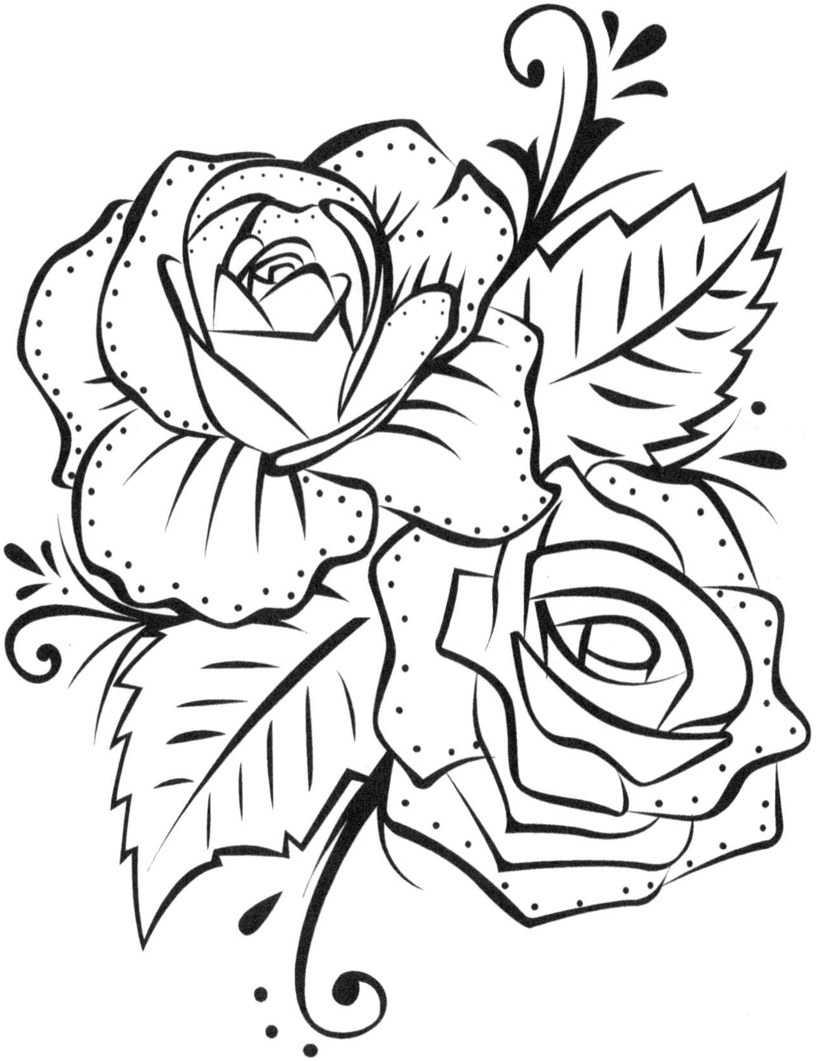

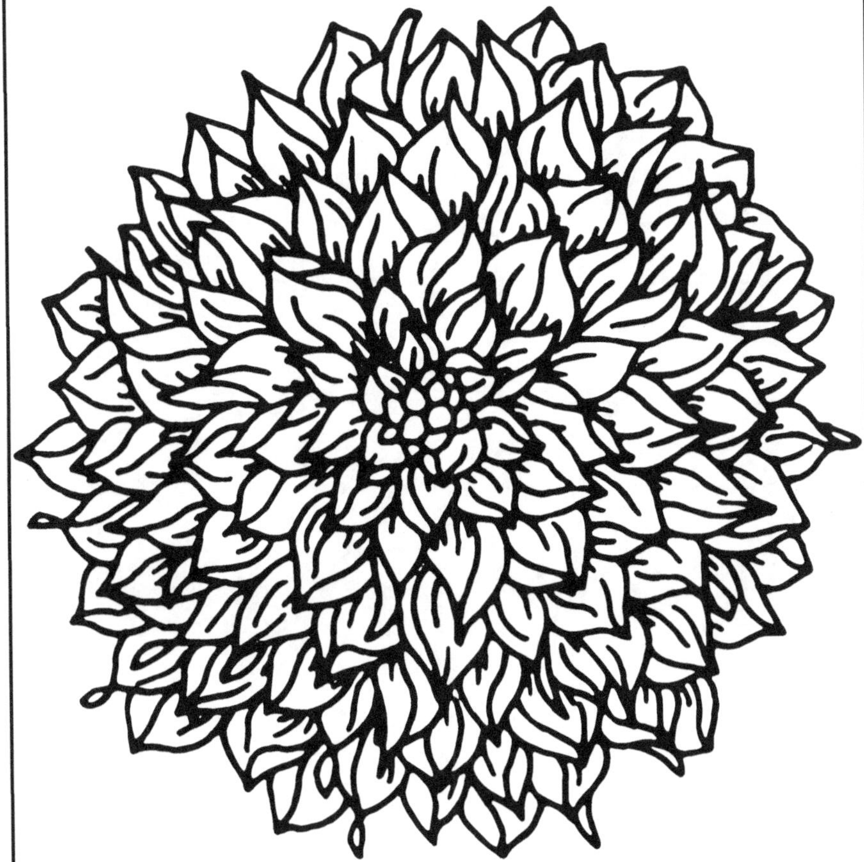

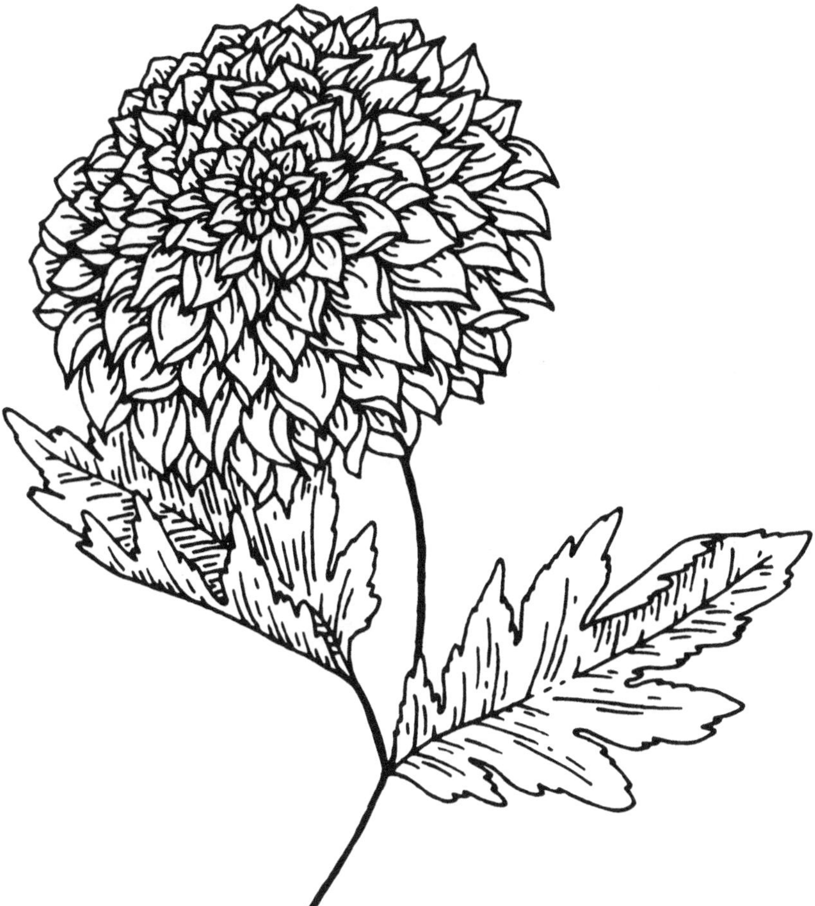

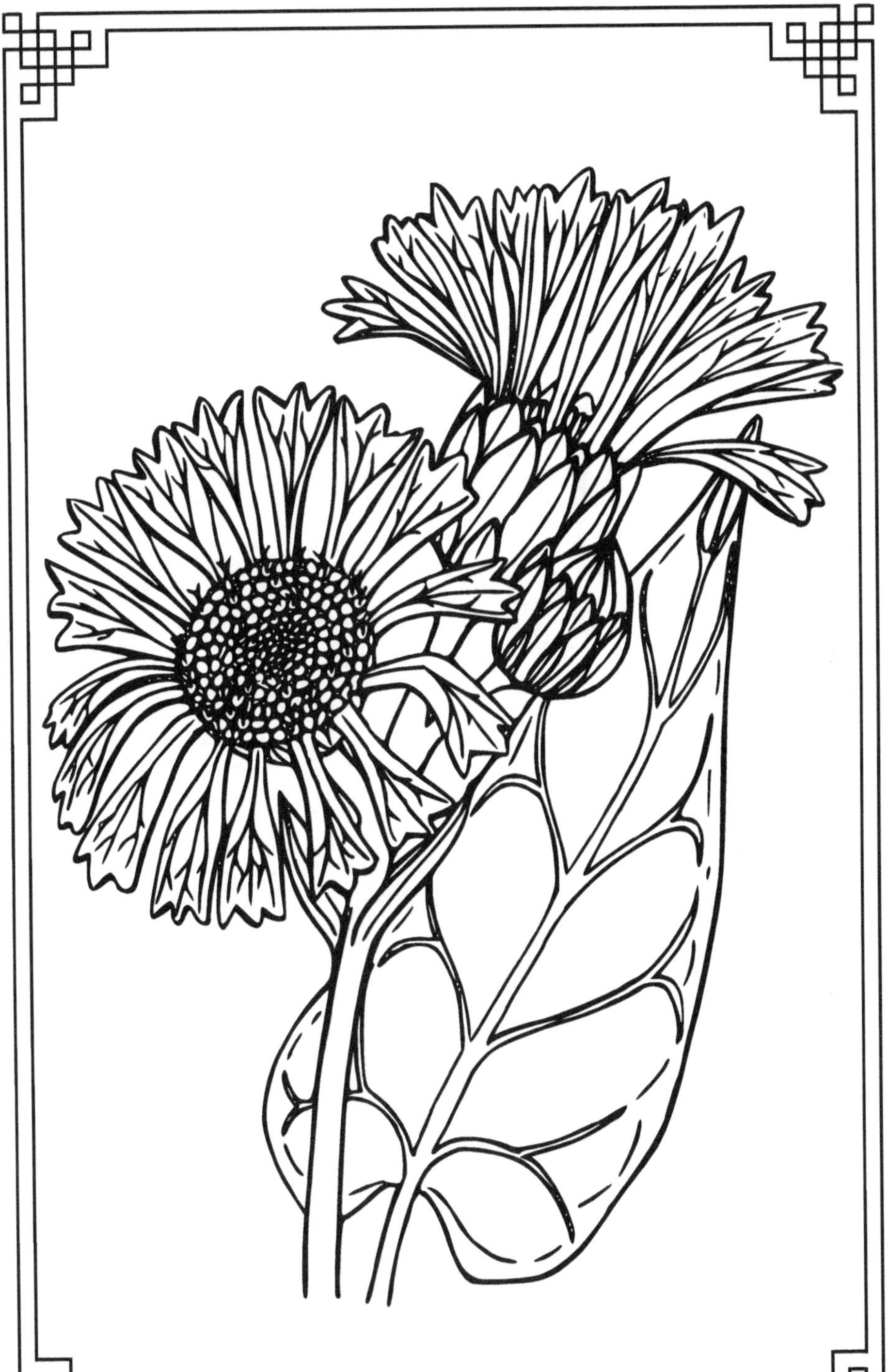

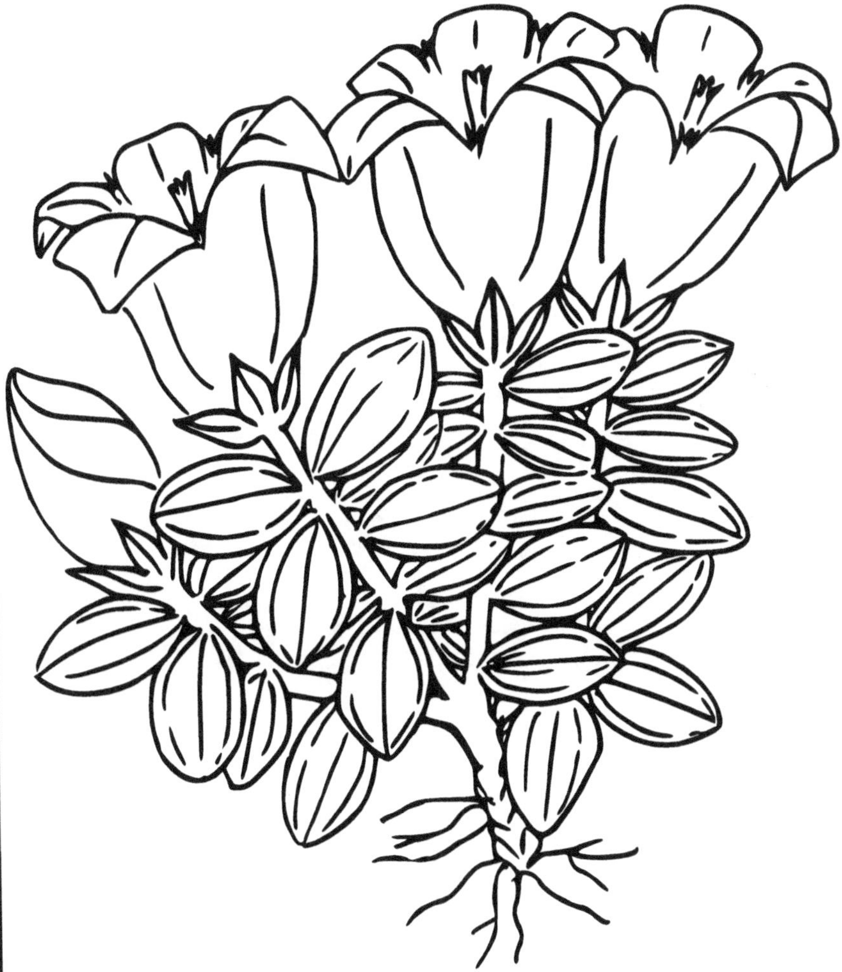

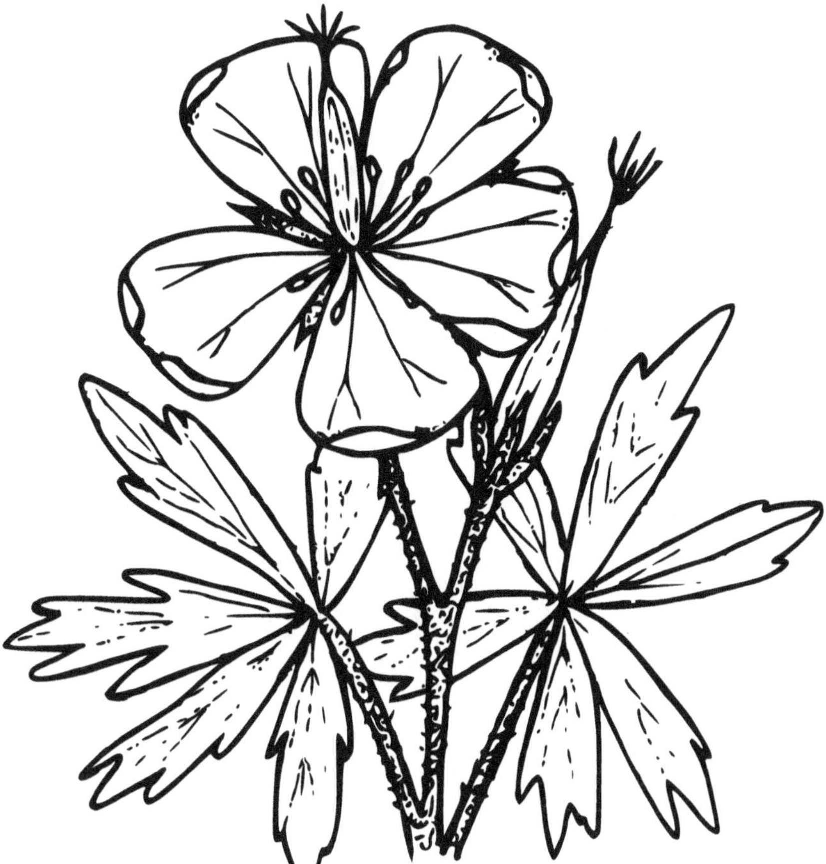

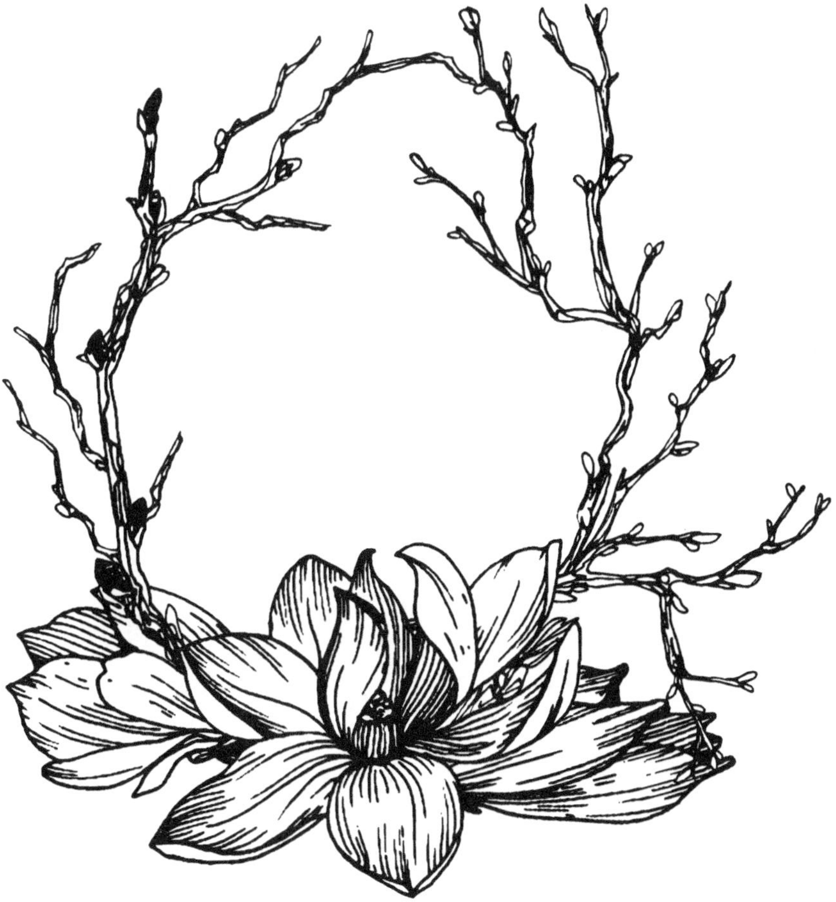

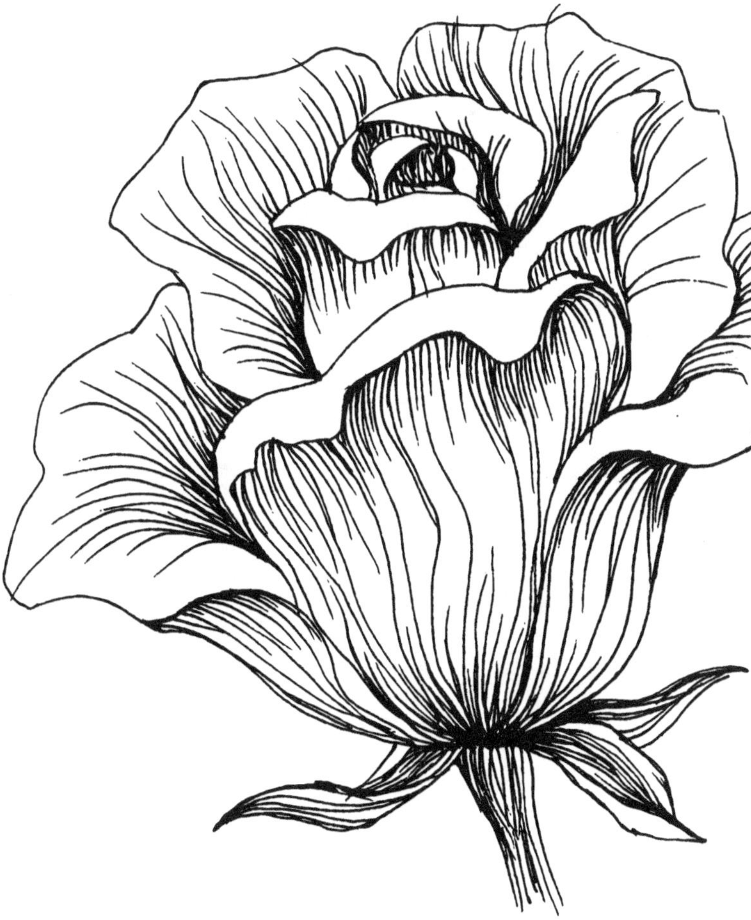

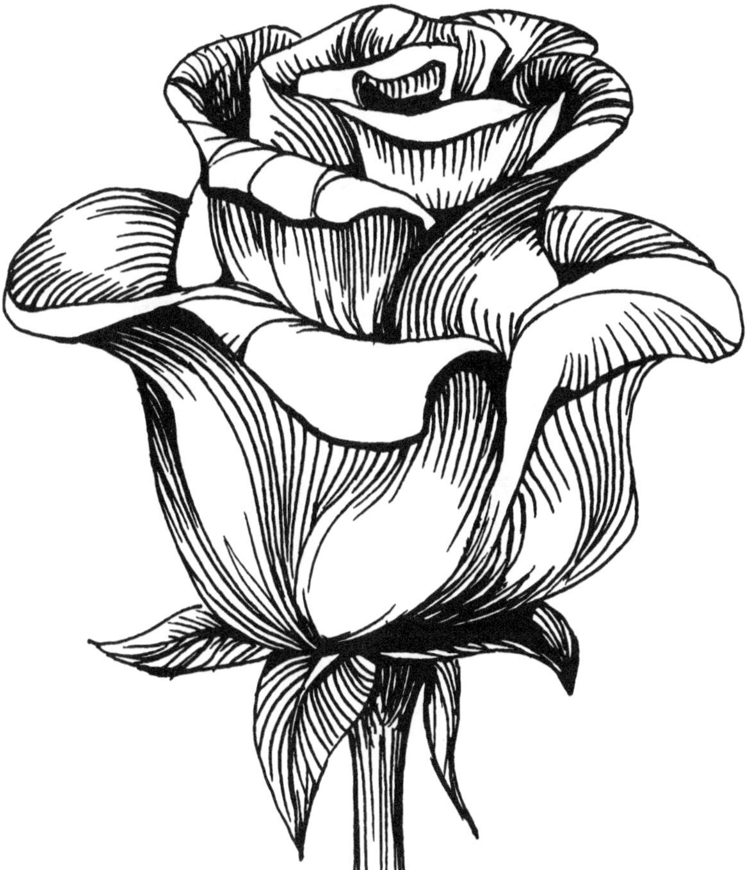

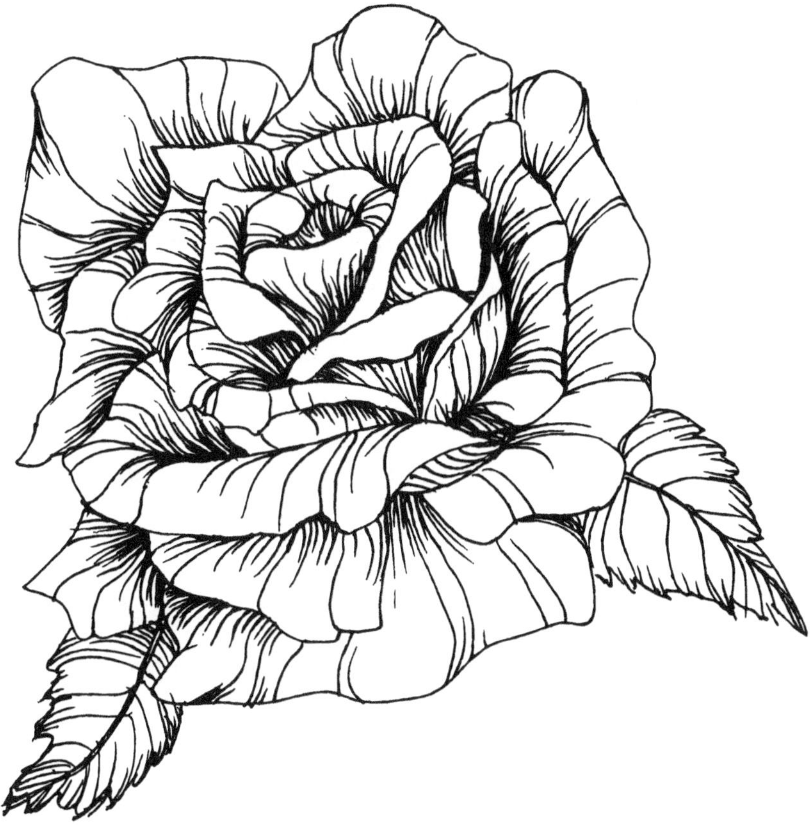

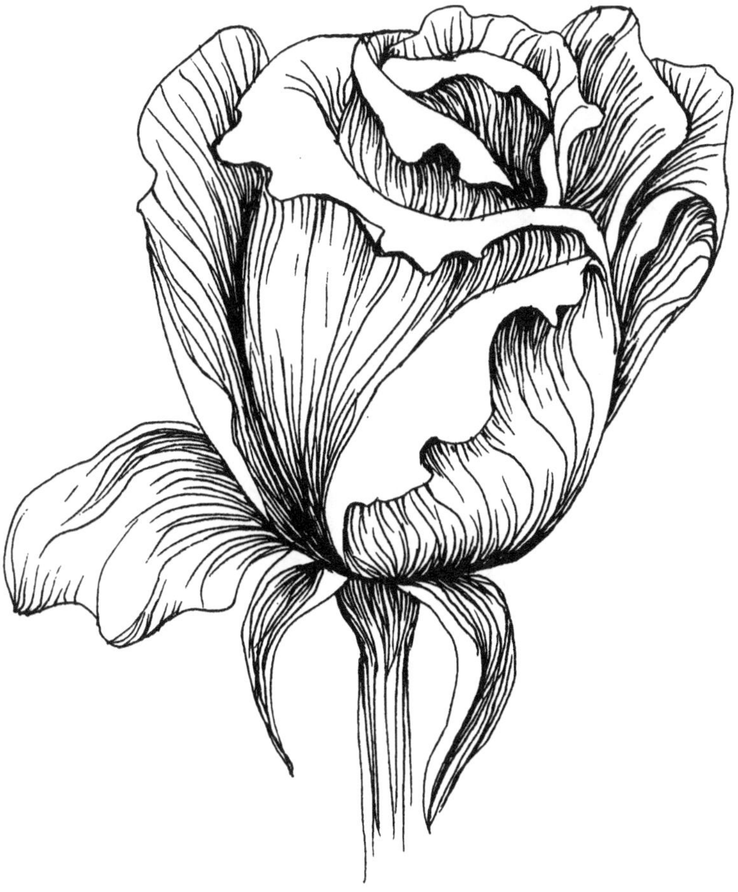

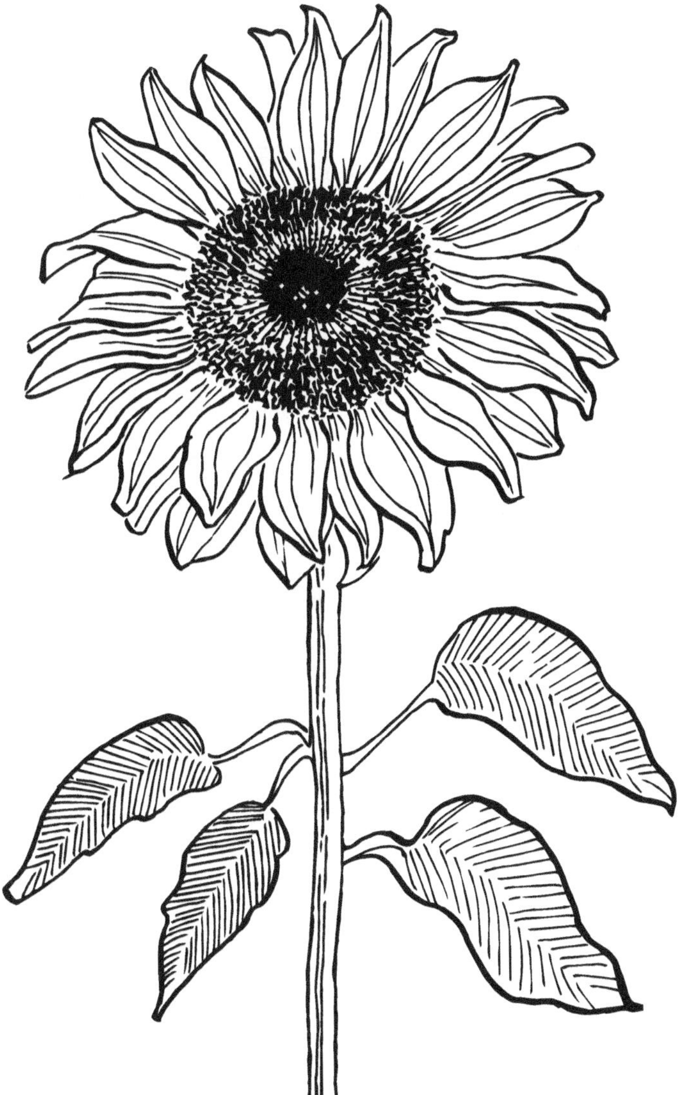

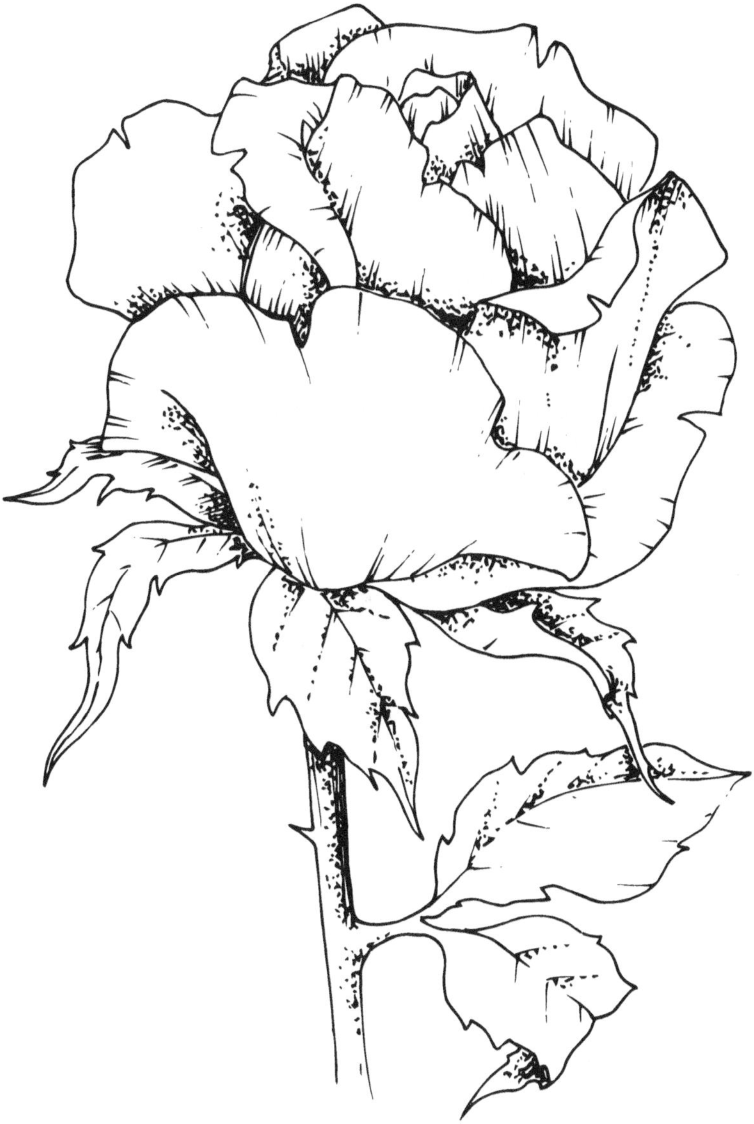

THANK YOU

www.ingramcontent.com/pod-product-compliance
Lightning Source LLC
Chambersburg PA
CBHW070131230526
45472CB00004B/1506
* 9 7 9 8 4 0 2 8 4 0 2 4 9 *